ASTOUNDING OPTICAL ILLUSIONS

KATHERINE
•JOYCE•

Nicholas Wade

Sterling Publishing Co., Inc. New York

Library of Congress Cataloging-in-Publication Data

Joyce, Katherine.
  Astounding optical illusions / Katherine Joyce.
      p.   cm.
  Includes index.
  ISBN 0-8069-0431-3
  1. Optical illusions—Juvenile literature.   [1. Optical
illusions.   2. Perception.]   I. Title.
  QP495.J68   1994
  153.7'4—dc20   93-43911
                                                         CIP
                                                          AC

Grateful acknowledgment is made for the illusions in "Optical Illusion Designs," taken from *The Art & Science of Visual Illusions* by Nicholas Wade, published by Routledge & Kegan Paul, London, England.

Line illustrations by Angelika Echsel

10   9   8   7   6   5   4   3   2   1

First paperback edition published in 1995 by
Sterling Publishing Company, Inc.
387 Park Avenue South, New York, N.Y. 10016
© 1994 by Katherine Joyce
Distributed in Canada by Sterling Publishing
% Canadian Manda Group, One Atlantic Avenue, Suite 105
Toronto, Ontario, Canada M6K 3E7
Distributed in Great Britain and Europe by Cassell PLC
Villiers House, 41/47 Strand, London WC2N 5JE, England
Distributed in Australia by Capricorn Link (Australia) Pty Ltd.
P.O. Box 6651, Baulkham Hills, Business Centre, NSW 2153, Australia
Manufactured in the United States of America
All rights reserved

Sterling ISBN 0-8069-0431-3 Trade
            0-8069-0432-1 Paper

Contents

Nicholas Wade

Before You Begin   **5**

1. Optical Illusion Designs   **7**

About Face · Cosmic Flower · Shimmering Squares · All Square · Making Waves · Tricky Tiles · Jester · Networking · Zinnia · Lattice · Square's Square · Spiral Square-Case · Squashed Circles · Seasick Circle · The Temple · The Escalator · Moire Grating · The Eternal Staircase · The Impossible Triangle · Chrysanthemum

2. Hidden Pictures   **28**

Showman's Wife · Cat · Bluebeard's Donkey · Cup · Giant · Landlord · Butler · Doctor · Mother Hubbard's Children · Rats · Dog's Master · Patient · Captain Webb · King · Milkmaid · Rabbit · Bird

3. Shadow Illusions   **38**

Duck · Pig · Weird Child · Rabbit · Evil Character · Goat · Elephant · Bird · Mule · Parrot · Dog's Face · Whole Dog · Old Man

4. Optical Illusion Tricks 43

Coin Magic · The Phantom Coin · The Tricky Pencil · The Mystery of the Shadowy Hand and the Disappearing Finger · The Big Catch · Make the Ball Disappear · Rebuild the Bridge · Creating Rainbows · The Rainbow Wheel · Colored Lights · Make a Color Viewing Box · Make a 3-D Viewer · Make Your Own Magnifying Glass

5. Illusion Magic 63

The Disappearing Scarf · The Rubber Pencil · Sticky Water

6. Tactile Illusions 69

The Muller-Lyer Illusion · Hot and Cold Water · Where Now? · Cross Your Fingers · The Curious Coin Trick · That Finger Weighs a Ton! · Doing the Twist · The Illusion of Weightlessness

7. Everyday Illusions 79

The Onion-Carrot Trick · Crazy Glass · What Do You Really Look Like? · The Doppler Effect · Wacky Wheels · Which Way? · Ping-Pong Blank Out · Down the Road · Mirages

Answers to Hidden Pictures 92

Index 96

Before You Begin

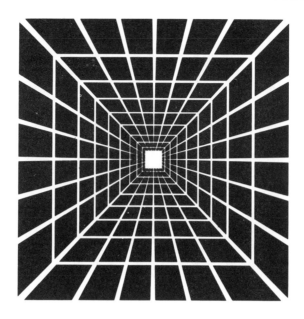

Nicholas Wade

This is a book of tricks for the eye and for the mind, so if you want to get the most out of it, have some fun with it.

Experiment with each illusion. Look at it with just one eye and see how your perception changes. Then turn the book upside down or sideways and see if the illusion looks any different. Show the illusion to your friends and find out if they see the same things you do.

Many of the optical illusions in this book work because they take advantage of basic weaknesses in the visual system. To understand what makes them work, you need to know a few things about how the visual system works.

Whenever you "see" an object, it is because light rays are reflected from the object through a lens in your eye. This lens is so flexible that you can focus on near

5

and far objects, and you can even see things that you're not really focusing on.

The light rays pass through your jelly-like eyeball and onto the retina—a screen at the back of your eye. The retina is made up of special cells that are sensitive to light and color. From the retina, visual messages are relayed to the brain along a pathway called the optic nerve.

Your brain then interprets this information into a picture.

The illusions that follow are just a few examples of the astounding gaps between the information that goes into our brains and the odd things that come out!

1. Optical Illusion Designs

About Face

Nicholas Wade

What do you see? Two upside-down faces? Or a fancy wine glass? This is one of the most familiar optical illusions. It relies on the fact that when you normally look at a picture, your brain uses the lines that form the outside of the drawing to differentiate it from the background. This is what tells you that you're looking at a picture of faces, for example.

But here, the same lines that form the edges of the faces also form the edges of a wine glass. So your eyes and brain have the choice of either seeing one picture or the other. Which image you see depends on the features of the picture that you're focusing on most strongly. In order to see the wine glass, you must see some parts of the lines as important and others as less important. And the other way around. As a result, it is impossible to see both the wine glass and the faces at the same time.

7

Cosmic Flower

Nicholas Wade

Take a look at the way this design pulsates. This is why:

When you look at anything that is close to you—this book, for example—the muscles around your eyes pull into a spherical shape to get the words and pictures in focus.

But because the lens of your eye isn't perfectly round, some parts of what you're looking at will be in focus and others will look blurry.

Normally, these differences in the clarity of your vision are on the outer edge of the object you're looking at, so you can still read the words and recognize the pictures. But in an illusion such as this one, where all the lines come from different angles and meet at the center, it is impossible for you to focus clearly on all of it at once.

Now, your eyes are always making tiny movements that you cannot prevent, no matter how hard you try. So the clear parts of the design and the blurry parts are constantly changing. This is called "optical distortion" and it's what makes the picture seem to move, shimmer, swirl or pulsate!

Optical distortion experiment

As an interesting experiment, try viewing "Cosmic Flower" or any of the other optical distortion illusions through a tiny hole punched in a piece of paper with a pin. Hold the paper close to your eye. You'll find that when you look through this "artificial pupil" the illusion appears dimmer and it doesn't move about nearly as much. This is because the light rays reflected from the design enter your eye straight through the hole and escape being distorted by the irregularities around the edge of your lens.

Shimmering Squares

The shimmering effect you'll see on the next page is caused by optical distortion. This illusion is unusual because all the lines in it are sloped either forward at 45° or backward at 135°. To see why this helps make the illusion more interesting, try the following experiment.

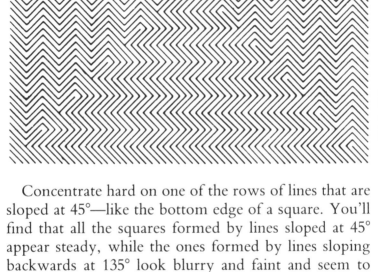

Nicholas Wade

Concentrate hard on one of the rows of lines that are sloped at 45°—like the bottom edge of a square. You'll find that all the squares formed by lines sloped at 45° appear steady, while the ones formed by lines sloping backwards at 135° look blurry and faint and seem to shimmer.

Then concentrate on a row of lines sloped at 135° and you'll see that all the squares formed with lines sloped at 45° will look blurry and faint and seem to shimmer.

This effect occurs because your eyes cannot focus on all of the illusion at once. The parts of the illusion that you do focus on will appear clear, while the parts of the illusion that are out of focus will look blurry.

All Square

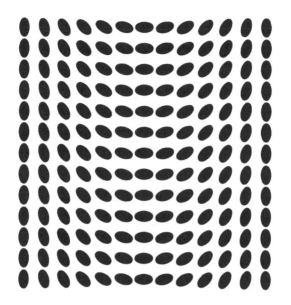

This optical illusion is especially puzzling. If you study it closely, the ovals in the middle first seem to bulge out and then they seem to recede.

The reason why they change out is that when your eyes scan the design from left to right, the position of the ovals suggests to your brain that the ovals are popping out. But then your eyes go back over the picture. With so many different ways to scan the illusion—and no clues to which way is "right"—you may see the ovals recede, or do any number of interesting tricks.

Making Waves

Nicholas Wade

When you stare at this optical illusion for a while, the curved lines seem to form the crests and valleys of waves. They may even seem to move a little. If you stare some more, until your eyes get tired, you may also see phantom lines of color, especially in bright light, where the curved lines run parallel to each other —between the valleys and crests of the waves.

The restless motion of the waves in this illusion is caused by optical distortion.

Tricky Tiles

Nicholas Wade

What makes this design vibrate? Right, it's optical distortion again! The repetition of the same design on each tile helps to make this illusion even more effective.

If all the swirling lines are making you seasick, try the experiment on page 9, viewing the illusion through an "artificial pupil."

Jester

Nicholas Wade

If you look at this circular checkerboard closely, it will seem to pulsate and shimmer. You may also see the black-and-white patches link up to form the petals of a flower.

The shimmering that you see is caused by optical distortion. But the petals formed by your brain are an example of another phenomenon called "good continuation." It happens because your brain is trying to make sense out of what it sees. It seeks out shapes or patterns that it recognizes. Sometimes it works so hard and so cleverly that it imagines an object that isn't really there. And then we have an optical illusion.

Networking

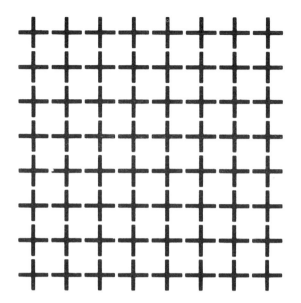

In this neat illusion, tiny white dots appear to join together to form phantom white crosses. This is another example of your brain trying to make sense of the visual information it is receiving—good continuation.

But there is another interesting phenomenon at work here. You can also see tiny grey dots in the center of the black crosses. Why? Special cells in your visual system respond strongly to small patches of light and dark. If a small light patch is surrounded by more light, these cells will not respond so strongly to the small patch of light in the middle. If a small dark patch is surrounded by more darkness, these cells will not respond so strongly to the small patch of dark in the middle.

So in the case of the black crosses, your visual system does not respond fully to the middle of them, and

— you see them as grey instead.

It doesn't have to be this way, though. You can force your eyes and brain not to "overlook" the midpoint of the crosses. If you focus your eyes and attention fully upon one cross at a time, you will be able to see it as an ordinary black cross.

Zinnia

Nicholas Wade

When you look at this illusion, you may see some grey or white spots at the points where the black lines meet. This is caused by your eyes' response to dark and light, as in "Networking."

And, if you go on studying this design, you may also see that these imaginary dots "link up" to form a series of circles that radiate out from the middle of the illusion. This is another example of good continuation.

Lattice

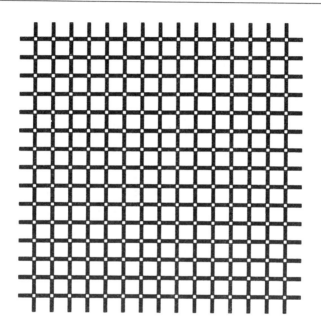

Here is an example of the role that contrast plays in your perceptions. Although there are only two colors used in this design—black and white—the tiny white dots in the middle, where the black lines intersect, seem brighter and whiter than the larger white squares. This is because the tiny white squares are more completely surrounded by the black lines than the larger white squares.

17

Square's Square

Nicholas Wade

This illusion may remind you of "Shimmering Squares," in which lines drawn at different angles confuse the brain. The squares here that have been drawn on the background pattern may look as if they have been bent, but in actual fact they are perfectly straight!

This is an example of the "Zollner effect." It shows how straight lines appear to bend if they intersect with or are seen against a background of curved lines or lines drawn at different angles. This strange effect occurs because your eyes and brain work together to try to make the straight lines fit into the background pattern.

18

Spiral Square-Case

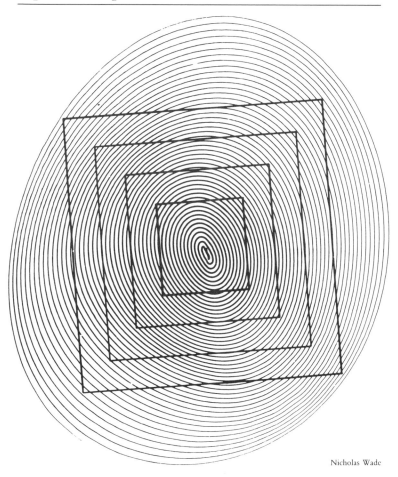

Nicholas Wade

The squares in the foreground look as if they are bent, right? Well, they do look that way. But this is another example of the Zollner effect. If you hold a ruler up alongside them, you'll see that the lines in the square are just as straight as they can be. It's only the curves of the spiral background that make the square seem bent.

Squashed Circles

Nicholas Wade

You can see all sorts of different effects when you look at this illusion. You may see flickering spokes radiating out from the central circle—turn the page from side to side to accentuate this effect. You can also view the central and smallest circle in two ways: as the top of a cone or as the end of a funnel.

The flickering spokes are a result of optical distortion.

Seasick Circle

Nicholas Wade

If you watch this drawing while you turn the book around in a circle, you will be able to see a series of spirals moving up and down in three dimensions.

This is what's called a "stereokinetic effect." It's the result of a complex series of interactions between your eyes and your brain.

When this design rotates, the images sent to your brain are constantly changing. Because each circle is drawn with lines that vary in thickness, there is no stable point in the illusion for you to focus on. This is confusing to your brain, which likes to make orderly patterns out of what it sees. So your brain looks for another pattern and sees that some of the curved lines seem to link up to form a spiral. As the curves that form the spiral rotate and change position, each of your eyes simultaneously sends your brain a slightly different image. When your brain puts this all together, it decides that it must be seeing a spiral moving up and down.

The Temple

This illusion combines two effects. It is a reversing figure: one way to look at it is as a pyramid viewed from above, with the smallest square forming the top. The other is as a passageway leading towards a tiny square door. If you look steadily at this illusion, you will probably see it flash between these two images.

It is also an example of optical distortion, because of the way it seems to shimmer.

22

The Escalator

Nicholas Wade

When you look closely at this optical illusion, you may get the impression that the horizontal panels are moving with a tiny jerking motion. The central panel may also seem unexpectedly bright. The reason that the "Escalator" appears to move is that, no matter how hard you try, you can't keep your eyes perfectly still, and as they move about, so do the images in the illusion.

Escalator experiment
To fully appreciate this illusion, ask a teacher or librarian to photocopy this picture onto a plastic film to

make a transparency. Place the transparency over the illusion and move it from side to side. You will experience the incredible "Moire effect" when the two patterns are superimposed.

You have undoubtedly observed the Moire effect before. It is in the patterns you see when two lace curtains overlap. They are produced where the thicker strands of the lace cross over each other to form a pattern.

You can also create a Moire effect using two combs. Hold them up to the light and slowly rotate one of the combs against the other. You will see a series of Moire fringes or bands appearing and disappearing.

Moire Grating

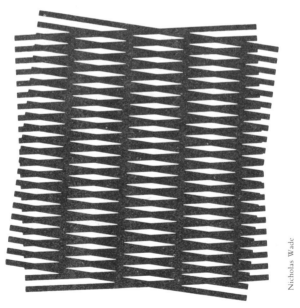

Nicholas Wade

This is one of the simplest types of Moire pattern, one formed by two identical gratings. The pattern you see is so strong that it is very difficult to see the path of each individual straight line. Try tracing the path of any straight black line with your finger and you'll see what I mean.

The Eternal Staircase

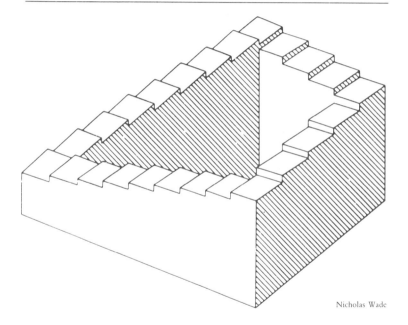

Nicholas Wade

Can you figure out which corner of the staircase is the highest? Probably not. Because this is not a real staircase—it's an "impossible figure." The drawing works because your brain recognizes it as three-dimensional. And a good deal of it is a realistic depiction. The first time you glance at it, the steps in "The Eternal Staircase" look quite logical. It is only when you look at the

25

drawing closely that you see that the entire structure is impossible.

"The Eternal Staircase" was first created by Lionel S. Penrose, a geneticist, and his son Roger. It later became known through the work of Maurits Escher, an artist who worked in the early part of the 20th century. Escher used many impossible figures such as this in his art, creating extremely odd paintings.

The Impossible Triangle

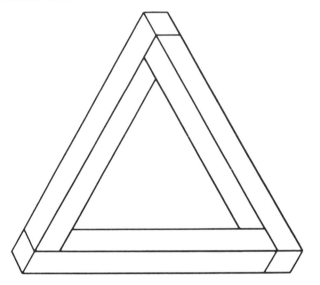

Nicholas Wade

Even if you were an expert carpenter, you'd never be able to construct this figure. Each of the three joints in the triangle is drawn with great accuracy. But the rods connecting them are not!

The fascinating thing about these illusions is that your brain is so convinced they are drawings of three-dimensional figures, that it is almost impossible to see them as the flat outline drawings they are.

26

Chrysanthemum

Nicholas Wade

When you look at this design, you get the impression that it is not flat, but three-dimensional. Some parts of the illusion appear higher and some lower, which gives the impression of depth. However, if you look at the curved lines that define the bumps and hollows of the flower, you will find a curious situation. Look at the curve that defines the outer edge of the flower, for instance, and follow it right around in a circle. You will see that in some places the curved lines seem to define a hump—and at others a hollow. This object could not exist in three dimensions. "Chrysanthemum" is another example of an impossible figure.

It also shimmers—so it is also a case of optical distortion.

2. Hidden Pictures

The picture puzzles in this section come from *Cole's Funny Picture Book,* a book by Edward William Cole that was published in the 1800s. Cole's book contains all sorts of stories, rhymes and funny pictures. But the most interesting things in the book are the picture puzzles, the best of which are reprinted here. These pictures may look ordinary enough, but they're really great examples of the art of illusion. If you didn't know that there were hidden pictures inside the pictures, you'd probably never know what you were missing.

For example, in this picture, some wild animals have gotten loose. Where is the bear?

So, look sharp and see just how many of the hidden faces, animals and people you can find. If you get really stuck, you'll find the answers to the picture puzzles at the back of this book.

He's up in the tree.

This is an easy one. Usually, you'll need to turn the book around and look harder.

---

1. Here is the Showman and his learned Dog. Where is his Wife?

2. Here are the Rats? Where is the Cat?

3. Here is Bluebeard and his Wife. Where is the Donkey?

4. Here is a lot of Furniture in a Room. Where is the Cup?

5. A Giant's Castle. Where is the Giant?

6. *Old Mother Hubbard. Find her Landlord.*

7. *Old Mother Hubbard. Find the Butler.*

8. Old Mother Hubbard. Find the Doctor.

9. Mother Hubbard with a few of her children. Where are her five other children?

10. Here is the Cat. Where are the Rats?

11. This is a Newfoundland Dog. Find his Master.

12. Here is the Nurse. Where is the Patient?

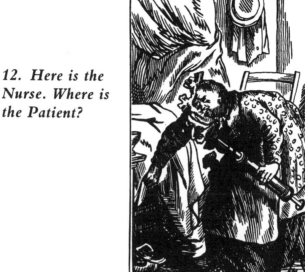

13. The Falls of Niagara. Find Captain Webb.

PUZZLE.
FIND
CAPTAIN WEBB.

14. The Queen is looking for His Majesty. Where is the King?

15. You can see the Goat plainly. Find the Milkmaid.

16. Here is the Cook. Where is the Rabbit?

17. Here is a Seashore. Where is the Bird?

3. Shadow Illusions

These shadow illusions also come from *Cole's Funny Picture Book*. To bring them to life, you need a blank wall and a reasonably bright, direct source of light that shines onto your hands.

It's always fun to make these fantastic shadow characters, but it's a specially good thing to do when you're sick in bed.

Once you've mastered some of the shadow illusions—or invented some of your own—you might like to put on a shadow play for your family and friends.

A good way to do this is to stretch an old white sheet across an open doorway. Turn on the light in the room in which you want to perform, and ask your audience to sit in the room on the other side of the sheet. It's best if the room in which your audience sits is dark—or only dimly lit.

To create special effects, such as the sun or a bonfire, get a friend to help by shining a flashlight with a colored filter on it (see "Colored Lights," pages 56–57).

1. Duck

2. Pig

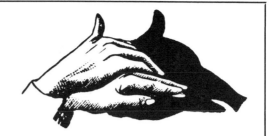

3. Weird Child

4. Rabbit

5. Evil Character

6. Goat

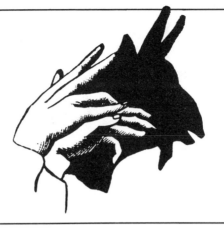

7. Elephant

8. Bird

9. Mule

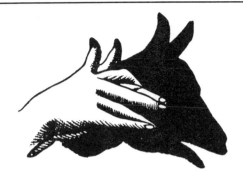

10. Parrot

11. Dog's Face

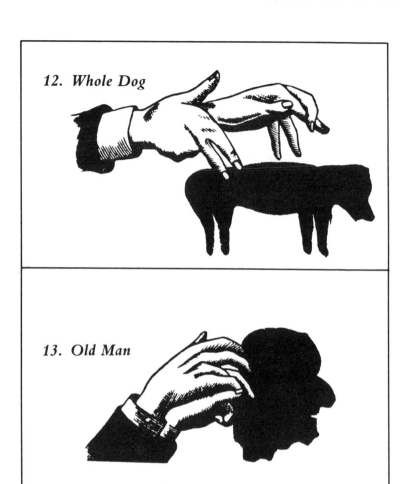

12. *Whole Dog*

13. *Old Man*

4. Optical Illusion Tricks

Coin Magic

Here's an experiment you might like to try with your friends.

You'll need
- *a bowl*
- *a coin*
- *some water*

How to do the trick
Place the bowl on a table and put the coin inside it. Now, back away from the table until you can no longer see the coin. As soon as the coin has disappeared from sight, stop moving and ask a friend to pour some water into the bowl. Amazingly, you can see the coin again!

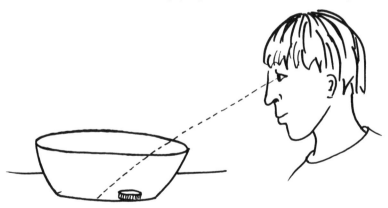

How the trick works
This trick relies on the fact that light travels more quickly through air than through water. When the light rays slow down as they enter the water, they also

change direction a little (see the diagram below). This allows you to see the coin again.

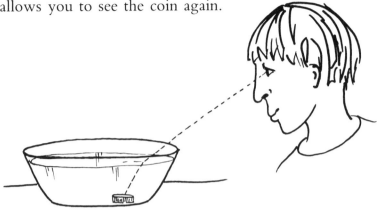

There is a special word to describe the way light appears to bend as it travels through different substances—refraction. It is refraction that makes the light rays look as if they bend at the point where the two substances meet. For another example of refraction, look at the way drinking straws seem to bend at the point where they enter the water in a glass.

The Phantom Coin

Imagine your friends' surprise when you show them that you cannot only turn one coin into two coins, but that you can make one of the coins float as well!

You'll need   •   *a glass*
            •   *water*
            •   *a saucer*
            •   *a coin*

How to do the trick
Fill a glass about ⅔ full of water and drop a coin into

44

the glass. Next, place a saucer over the glass and carefully turn the glass over. Invite your friends to look down into the glass. Incredibly, they will see not one coin, but two—one resting on the saucer at the "bottom" of the glass, and one floating on top of the water!

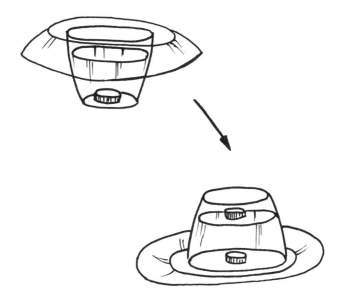

How the trick works

The reason you see two coins when only one coin really exists also has to do with the way light bends when it travels through different substances.

When the light rays reflected by the coin leave the water, they bend slightly before they enter your eye. However, your brain doesn't know that. When you see that phantom coin floating near the top of the water, it is because your brain has created an image of the coin where the light rays *would have come from* if they had not been bent.

The Tricky Pencil

You'll need • *a clean glass*
• *water*
• *a pencil with a flat top*

How to do the trick
Fill a clean glass with water and place it on a table. Take a pencil and stand it on the top of the table about a foot (30cm) behind the glass. Now look through the glass of water. You'll see not one but two pencils!

Close your right eye and look through the glass of water again. You'll see only one pencil.

Open your right eye and close your left eye. How many pencils do you see this time?

Now open both eyes, look through the glass another time, and you'll see two pencils again.

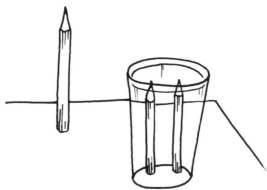

How the trick works
Because the glass is shaped like a cylinder, each eye looks through the water at a slightly different angle. So, when you have both eyes open, each eye sees a slightly different image of the pencil—and you see two pencils. When you have only one eye open, you see only one image of the pencil.

46

The Mystery of the Shadowy Hand and the Disappearing Finger

Check out this simple trick that befuddles your eyes and brain into seeing images that aren't really there.

How to do the trick
Hold your left hand up at arm's length in front of your face while you focus on an object about three or four feet (1m–1.2m) away. Part of a shadowy hand will appear just to the right of your left hand.

Now, still looking at that object with your left hand out in front of you, raise your right hand, extending your index finger closer and closer to your left hand, until your fingertip disappears behind it. But is your finger really hidden behind that hand? Look at your hands

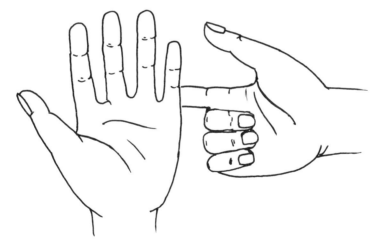

and see. You'll find that you haven't really moved your right index finger behind your left hand—it only looks that way when you focus on the distant point. In reality, your finger will still be about half an inch (1.25cm) away from your left hand!

How the trick works

When you focus on a point about four feet (1.2m) away, the image of your hand and finger (which are only a short distance from you) becomes blurry. When you bring your index finger closer towards your left hand, the images from your right eye and your left eye overlap. As a result, your fingertip seems to disappear.

The Big Catch

How to do the trick

Pick up this book and hold it so that your nose touches the dot between the baseball and the mitt. Now, turn the book slowly in a counterclockwise direction. You will see the ball fly up in a graceful arc and land in the mitt! Congratulations! You made the big catch!

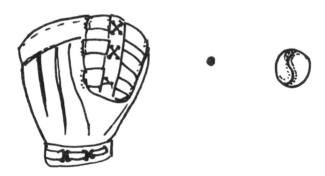

How the trick works

You already know that each of your eyes sees a slightly different picture. Close your right eye and focus on an object about three feet (1m) away from you, such as a clock or a poster. Now, quickly open your right eye and close your left. The object you're looking at will seem to change its position slightly—it may even seem to jump. Then close your right eye and open your left eye again. The object will appear to be in the same place as before.

So, now you've seen for yourself how you see a slightly different image with each eye. When you look at an object with both eyes at the same time, your brain processes both images into a single picture. When you look at the picture of the baseball and the mitt, your left eye sees the mitt, and your right eye sees the ball. When your brain combines these two images, the ball appears to sail into the mitt.

Make the Ball Disappear

This little ghost fancies himself as a magician. With your help, he will make the ball disappear, and then appear again.

All you need to do is hold this book at a normal reading distance from your face and close your left eye. Now focus on the ghost's magic wand with your right eye and very slowly move the book towards your face. At one point, the ball will disappear.

49

How the trick works

Doing this trick, you have actually discovered your "blind spot." That is a point at the back of each of your eyes where your optic nerve joins the retina (that screen at the back of your eye). Most of the surface of the retina is made up of cells called "rods" and "cones." These are sensitive to light and color. However, there are none of these cells at the point where your optic nerve joins the retina, so you cannot see the light rays that are reflected onto it.

In order to find the blind spot at the back of your right eye, redraw this picture so that the ghost is on the right-hand side of the ball and repeat the experiment with your right eye closed, staring at the magic wand with your left eye as you slowly bring the page closer to your face.

Rebuild the Bridge

The bridge in the picture has been damaged and the middle section of the roadway is missing. Fortunately, it's very simple to repair. Just hold the page so that the gap in the bridge is directly in front of you and bring the book towards your face until the white gap touches your nose. At one point, the gap will close.

This illusion relies on one important fact for its success. That is, when you look at something with both eyes open, you actually see two images of the object. Your brain puts them together and interprets them as a single object.

How big or small that object seems to be depends on how far away from you it is. A person who is a long distance away might appear as small as an ant, even though that same person, if he were standing beside you, might be bigger and taller than you are.

When you slowly bring the page of this book closer to your face, the image formed by each eye gradually gets bigger. Eventually, each image is so large that the two pictures overlap and the bridge seems—mysteriously—to repair itself.

You can prove to yourself that the two images produced by your eyes rebuild the bridge. Just close one eye and bring the book closer and closer to your face until it touches your nose. Instead of seeing the two halves of the bridge meet, you'll just see one side of the bridge—and your nose!

Creating Rainbows

There is more than one way to create a rainbow, depending on the weather, the time of day and the equipment on hand.

How to do the trick
1. On a bright, sunny day, try the following technique:

You'll need
- *a bowl*
- *water*
- *a small, flat mirror*
- *a piece of cardboard*

First, fill the bowl with water. Then take the mirror and rest it inside the bowl. Place the bowl and mirror in front of a window, or in some other place where rays of sunlight will strike the mirror. Hold the cardboard in front of the mirror, moving it around until a rainbow appears on it.

If you can't see a rainbow, adjust the position of the mirror. With a little trial and error, you'll soon create a rainbow inside your own home.

2. When the sun is low in the sky, in the morning or evening, you can make a rainbow using the following method.

You'll need • *a glass with smooth sides*
• *water*
• *a piece of white paper*

Find a window that has sunlight streaming through it, and place the glass nearby so that the sun shines through it. You could place it on a windowsill, on a table or on a chair. Fill the glass completely full of water, and then put a sheet of white paper on the floor beneath it. A rainbow will appear on the paper.

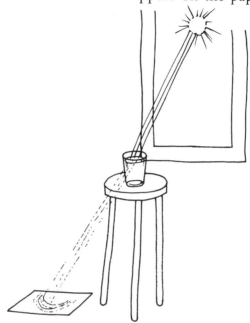

3. A third way that you can create a rainbow during the early morning or late afternoon is with a garden hose outside in the garden. Turn on the hose and adjust the nozzle, or put your thumb over the end of the hose, so that the water comes out in a spray of very fine droplets. Now stand in front of some dark shrubs with your back to the sun and you will see a rainbow.

How these tricks work
In nature, a rainbow is created when sunlight strikes tiny droplets of water that are suspended in the air. These drops act like prisms and split the sunlight into the individual colors that make up the white light.

When you create your own rainbow using the first method, the water acts as a prism.

In the second experiment, the rim of the glass of water acts as a prism.

In the third experiment, the droplets of water act as a prism to split up the light, just as they do when you see a rainbow in the sky.

All these experiments prove that sunlight, which we see as white, is actually made up of rays of different colors—red, orange, yellow, green, blue, indigo (a blue-purple) and violet. (Sunlight also contains ultra-violet and infrared rays, but these are invisible to humans.)

All of these rays of light travel at slightly different speeds, so they are each refracted (bent) a slightly different amount by the prism. This is what allows us to see the separate colors.

The Rainbow Wheel

There's no real trick to this trick—it simply demonstrates that white light is made up of the seven colors of the rainbow. It's a fascinating thing to see, though, so we've included it in this book as part of the magic of everyday life that we take for granted.

You'll need
- *scissors*
- *a piece of cardboard*
- *a protractor*
- *colored pencils, crayons or paint*
- *a sharp pencil*

How to do the trick
Take scissors and cut out a circle with a diameter of about four inches (10cm) from the cardboard. Then,

with the protractor, divide the circle up into seven equal sections. Each section will be about 51° wide.

Color each section with one of the colors of the rainbow so that your cardboard disc looks like this:

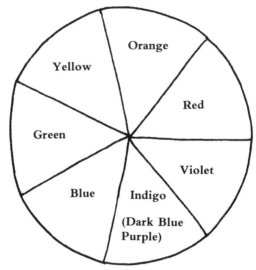

Then make a small hole in the middle of the disc and push a sharp pencil through it.

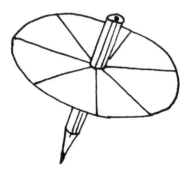

Finally, spin the pencil quickly on a hard surface so that the disc moves very rapidly. You see WHITE! Isn't it amazing?

Colored Lights

When you read through this experiment, before you actually try it for yourself, you may find it hard to believe what's going to happen. Mixing colored beams of light is totally different from mixing colored paints.

You'll need
- *3 flashlights*
- *3 sheets of cellophane, one red, one blue and one green*
- *3 rubber bands for fastening the cellophane over the flashlights*
- *a screen or white paper or white wall*

Since this trick requires a lot of equipment that you probably don't have at home, it may be a good idea to get together with two friends so that each one can supply a flashlight and a sheet of cellophane. This trick would also make a really neat group science project for school.

How to do the trick

First, fasten a piece of cellophane over the light end of each one of the flashlights with the rubber bands. You will now have flashlights that give out red, blue and green light.

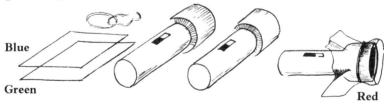

Next, find a suitable room to perform this experiment in. It should be as dark as possible. Put a blanket over the windows, if necessary. If the room has white walls you can shine your flashlight right at the wall. If not, you may need to use white paper or a movie screen if you have one.

Begin your light show by shining the flashlight with the red cellophane and the one with the blue cellophane at different places on the white wall.

Now direct the flashlight beams on the middle of the wall, so that the two beams of light overlap. The purple color that you will see is called magenta. You may have seen this color while using the "paint box" of a computer.

Next, shine the blue and green beams so that they overlap. The blue-green color that you will see is called cyan. This is another color that you may have seen on a computer screen.

Now shine the red and green beams together. What color do you see? SURPRISE! I bet you didn't expect that red and green flashlight beams would combine to make yellow!

Finally, shine the flashlights at the screen so that the three different colors all overlap. What color do you see in the middle of the pool of light? You'll probably be very surprised to see that the area where all three colored beams of light overlap is actually white!

How the trick works

Red, blue and green are known as the primary colors of light. Yes, that's different from paint, where the primary colors are red, blue and yellow.

Magenta, cyan and yellow—the colors that you see when you "mix" the primary colors together two-by-two—are known as the secondary colors of light.

All these colors have light waves that travel at slightly different speeds. When blue, red and green lights are mixed all together, their separate wavelengths combine to form white light.

Make a Color Viewing Box

When is a green apple no longer a green apple? When does a juicy red tomato no longer look red? When you view them through a viewing box with a red filter, of course.

You'll need
- *a shoebox (or a similar cardboard box with a lid)*
- *scissors*
- *extra cardboard*
- *sticky tape*
- *cellophane (red, green and blue)*
- *a green apple*
- *a red tomato*

How to do this trick

The first thing you need to do is construct the viewing box. Cut a small hole, about 1½ inches (3.75cm) in diameter in one of the narrow ends of the box. This is your viewing hole.

Next, cut a rectangular hole in the middle of the lid of the box. This hole should be about 3½ inches (8.75cm) long and 2½ inches (6.25cm) wide.

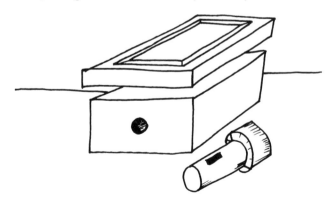

Finally, make the color filters. Cut rectangular frames out of the cardboard and tape a piece of cellophane across each one. The frames should be about four inches (10cm) long by three inches (7.5cm) wide so that they cover the hole in the top of the box. Use the red, blue and green cellophane to make the filters.

To use your viewing box, first place the object you are going to look at in the box underneath the color filter. Then look through the viewing hole at the end of the box while you shine a flashlight through the colored filter at the top of the box.

When you look at the green apple while shining your flashlight through the red filter, it will look dark. When you look at the red tomato, it will appear pale.

How the trick works

The red filter on top of the box allows only red light rays to enter the box. The red tomato appears pale because it can reflect only the red light that passes through the filter.

As for the apple, the red filter prevents green light from entering the viewing box. Since the green apple reflects mostly green light rays, it appears dark.

When all the colored wavelengths of light are kept out, the interior of the box becomes much dimmer. This fact is important because the cone-shaped cells in the retina, which are sensitive to color, work best in bright light.

You may have noticed that in a dark room, you can't see color at all: everything you see is in shades of grey. Or you may have walked into a dim room and noticed that normally bright colors appeared pale. This is what happens when you look at the red tomato when it's under the red filter. It appears pale because the dimness of the red light in the box prevents the cones in your retina from responding fully.

As for the apple, the red filter on the top of the viewing box prevents green light from entering the box, and since the green apple cannot reflect the red light, it appears dark.

Make a 3-D Viewer

Two-dimensional images drawn on a flat piece of paper can look as if they are three-dimensional with this simple 3-D viewer.

You'll need
- *a piece of paper or cardboard*
- *a ruler*
- *scissors*
- *a picture or photo*

How to make the viewer

Draw a cross in the middle of the cardboard. The vertical part of the cross should be about 2 inches (5cm) high and half an inch (1.25cm) wide. Each arm of the cross should be about ¾ of an inch (2cm) long and half an inch (1.25cm) wide.

Using a ruler, make sure that the lines are neatly drawn. Then, with scissors, cut out the cross and remove it, leaving a window in the piece of cardboard.

Next, place the picture or photo that you want to view flat on a table. Pictures of objects with lots of straight lines, such as buildings, work best. Place the cardboard upright at right angles to the picture.

Now stare down hard through the cross for a few seconds and you'll see the picture stand out in three dimensions.

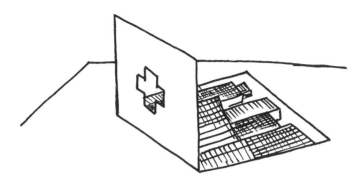

How the trick works
First, the cross hides the edges of the picture, keeping you from seeing that it's really flat. Second, your brain is used to seeing the world in three dimensions, so it automatically creates a three-dimensional image for you. We really do see what we expect to see!

Make Your Own Magnifying Glass

Challenge your friends with this simple scientific trick.

You'll need
- *a straw*
- *a small piece of cardboard*
- *a cup of water*
- *scissors*
- *clear sticky tape*
- *a sheet of newspaper*

How to do the trick

Place all the materials on a table and challenge your friends to use them to make the letters on the newspaper look bigger than they actually are—to create a magnifying glass, in effect.

If you want, you can stop reading right here and try to figure out how to do the trick yourself.

How the trick works

With the scissors, cut a circle about an inch (2.5cm) in diameter in the piece of cardboard. Now place a piece of sticky tape over the hole. Using the straw, carefully put a drop of water on the tape. Now look closely at the newspaper through the drop of water. You'll see that the letters do look bigger. You have made your own personal magnifying glass!

When you look at an object through a drop of water, it will look bigger than it really is. That's because the drop of water acts as a lens, a convex lens. A convex lens is thicker in the middle and thinner at the edges—it bulges out. A convex lens refracts (bends) light waves so that objects seem to be bigger than they actually are.

5. Illusion Magic

The Disappearing Scarf

This is a fun little trick in which you show your audience an ordinary silk scarf and a paper bag. Then you blow a few breaths of air into the paper bag and put the scarf inside it. Finally you blow up the paper bag until it looks like a balloon. Then you burst the paper bag. Incredibly, the scarf inside doesn't fall out of the bag—it has mysteriously disappeared!

You'll need
- *a silk scarf or a large handkerchief that can be crumpled easily into a small ball*
- *2 paper bags*
- *scissors*
- *glue*

How to do the trick
First you need to make a special paper bag with a secret compartment. You need two paper bags to do it. Take a scissors and cut the bottom third off one of the paper bags, as in #1. Glue this false bottom onto one side of the inside of the other paper bag (#2). Wait for the glue to dry and you'll be ready to do the trick.

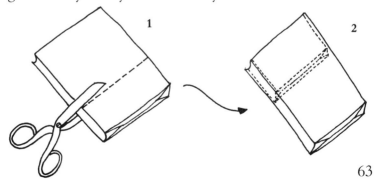

When you perform this trick, open the paper bag so that your audience cannot see inside it. Then blow gently into it to inflate it. When you take the silk scarf out of your pocket, put it into the secret compartment at the top of the paper bag (#3). Blow into the bag a few more times until it is fully inflated. Then burst the bag and listen to your audience gasp when they discover that the scarf has disappeared!

The Rubber Pencil

The Effect
You take a pencil out of your pocket and, holding it firmly in both hands, explain to your audience that this is a very weird pencil that sometimes does strange and unpredictable things. Then you take one hand off the pencil so that you are holding it by only one end. You give the pencil a few quick jerks. Suddenly, as if jolted into life, the pencil begins to bend and wiggle as if it were made of rubber.

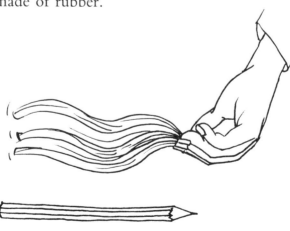

How to do the trick

The pencil that you use in this trick is just an ordinary pencil. To make it look as if it's made of rubber, simply grasp it with your right thumb and first finger, and, holding it horizontally, wiggle it with short, quick shakes. It will appear to bend without your having to do anything "magical."

How the trick works

You can move the pencil faster than the people in the audience can see it. You'll remember that, in order for you to see anything, light waves from the object first have to travel through your eye until they hit the screen at the back of your eye called the retina. The cells of the retina respond to the light waves and send a message along the optic nerve to your brain. Your brain then interprets the visual information from both eyes into a single picture of whatever it is you are looking at. The brain is able to process many of these images every second, so that you get a smooth, uninterrupted flow of vision. However, the brain cannot process these images fast enough to keep up with your wiggling pencil! It is just wiggling too fast!

So when your friends look at the wiggling pencil, instead of seeing a single image of the pencil every time it moves a tiny bit up or down in the air, they see the many possible positions of the pencil, all combined into a blurry set of images.

You've probably noticed this before when you watched the blades of an electric fan or the propeller of a plane.

Sticky Water

Who ever heard of water that sticks to the sides of a bottle and doesn't come out, even if the bottle is held upside down? No, there isn't a top on the bottle. I'll bet you've never seen this, and probably none of your friends will have either—until you show them this amazing trick that defies the force of gravity!

The Effect
You show your audience a small glass soft-drink bottle about ¾ full of water. Next, you tell them that if you put exactly the right amount of water in a bottle, it will not pour out.

Your friends watch as you hold the bottle upside down with your right hand and drops of water spill out over your left hand and into the bowl below. Suddenly, they realize that there is no more water trickling out of the bottle, and there's nothing to hold it in there either! It's as if the water has suddenly gotten sticky and is stuck to the sides of the bottle.

"There, you see?" you say.

Then, as your friends sit spellbound, you suddenly hit the bottom of the bottle with your left hand, and the rest of the water pours out into the bowl below.

You'll need   • *scissors*
   • *a sheet of cellophane*
   • *glass soft-drink bottle*
   • *pencil (optional)*

How to do the trick
With the scissors, cut a disc in the cellophane that is the same size as the mouth of the soft-drink bottle. When

you perform the trick, have this disc lying on your table beside the bottle. (You could also moisten the disc with water and stick it on the fingers of your left hand in advance.)

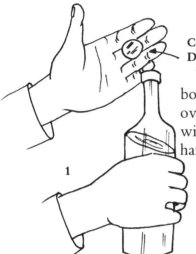

Cellophane Disc

While you are still holding the bottle right-side up, slide the disc over the mouth of the bottle with the fingers of your left hand (#1).

When you turn the bottle upside down, spread the fingers of your left hand very carefully, and smooth the cellophane over the mouth of the bottle. The edges of the disc will seal themselves against the bottle (#2).

When you remove your fingers, the cellophane will hold the water in place.

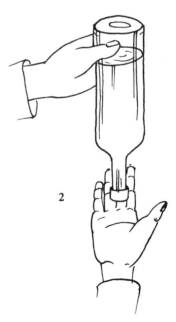

After your audience has had a good look at the bottle of sticky water, hit the bottom of the bottle to dislodge the disc and let the water pour out (#3). Or, if you'd rather, poke a pencil inside the bottle to "loosen the water."

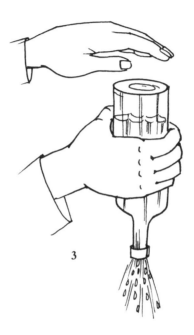

3

How the trick works
The air pressure surrounding the bottle is greater than the air pressure inside it. This is what holds the cellophane to the mouth of the bottle.

Have fun with this one!

Note: The mouth of the bottle should not be wider than two of your fingers.

6. Tactile Illusions

The Muller-Lyer Illusion

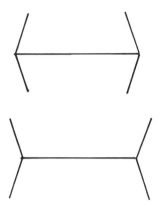

Which of these two lines do you think is longer? If you were to take a guess, you'd probably choose the bottom line. However, you'd be wrong. The bottom line does look longer, but, in actual fact, both horizontal lines are exactly the same length.

This illusion was named after the two men who discovered it, and it is one of the most puzzling of all the illusions, because it is not only an optical illusion, but it also works on a tactile level—the level of touch.

To prove to yourself that your sense of touch can be fooled by this remarkable illusion, you need to construct the object below.

You'll need
- *thick, stiff cardboard (not the corrugated kind)*
- *strong glue (paste or glue sticks are not good enough)*
- *scissors*

Begin by cutting a strip of cardboard twice as long as one of the horizontal lines in the illusion above. This strip of cardboard should be one inch (2.5cm) wide. Do this as accurately as you can. Then cut six smaller pieces of cardboard to form the "arrows" on the end of each part of the line. These should be as long as one side of the arrow shown in the visual illusion, and one inch (2.5cm) wide. Glue these small pieces of cardboard onto the long piece of cardboard so that you have made something that looks like the object below.

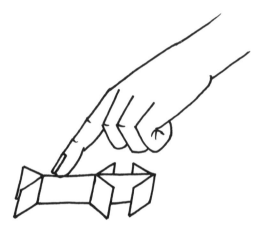

Check carefully to make sure that the angles formed by the "V" of each of the arrows are all the same size. Remember also to check that the "arrows" placed in the middle of the figure are exactly in the middle.

Then leave the object to dry.

When the cardboard illusion is completely dry, explore and compare the two parts. You'll find that your fingers come to the same conclusion that your eyes do: the section of the puzzle that has the arrows pointing inward seems to be longer than the other section of the puzzle.

How the trick works

One explanation of why the Muller-Lyer illusion works visually has been proposed by Richard Gregory, who published the results of his work on illusions in the 1970s. Using special tests for estimating distance, Gregory found that observers see the lines as symbolic of other objects. To see for yourself how Gregory came to this conclusion, turn this book around so that the straight lines are vertical. You will see that the line with the arrows pointing outward resembles a corner of the outside of a building. The line with the arrows pointing inward looks like the distant inside corner of a room. Since the vertical line of the room appears to be farther away, your visual system assumes that the line is longer than it appears to be, in order to compensate for it being in the distance.

However, this doesn't explain why the illusion works when the lines are horizontal, and it doesn't explain why the tactile illusion works.

Another theory about the Muller-Lyer illusion is the "eye movements" theory. It goes like this: when you look at the lines at the top of page 69, the bottom line seems longer because your eyes have to scan beyond the ends of the straight line in order to see the whole figure—including the arrows at the end. So your eyes have to scan a greater horizontal distance. It may be that the tactile illusion works in a similar way. Your fingers have to reach beyond the length of the straight line between the two arrows in order to touch all of this section of the puzzle. This may give us an exaggerated sense of the length of this part of the object.

Hot and Cold Water

One of the best parts of this trick is the surprise, so when you try it out on your friends, don't tell them what's going to happen.

How to do the trick
First, find three bowls or pots that are large enough for you to put your hands in. Fill the first bowl with cold water straight from the tap. Fill the second bowl with hot water—as hot as a hot bath, but no hotter. Fill the third bowl with lukewarm water—water that feels neither hot nor cold.

Place one hand in the bowl of cold water and one hand in the bowl of hot water for one minute. When the minute is up, remove your hands from both the bowls and put them in the bowl of lukewarm water. When you do this, you will experience an amazing effect. The hand that was soaking in the hot water will not feel cold, and the hand that was soaking in the cold water will now feel hot!

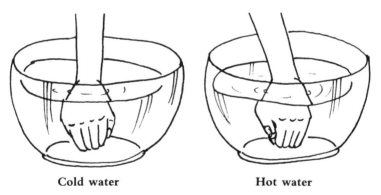

Cold water   Hot water

How the trick works
It works because your sense of touch relies on comparing things in order to figure them out.

72

If, for example, you have never slept on anything but a soft, mushy bed, a bed that is rated "medium" might seem hard to you. However, that same bed might seem soft to another person who has always slept on a firm bed. So, to the hand that was soaking in the hot water, the lukewarm water seems so much colder that your hand sends a message to your brain saying that it's cold. And to the hand that was soaking in the cold water, the lukewarm water feels so nice and warm by contrast that it sends your brain a message saying that it's hot.

That's why each of your hands tells you that the same bowl of lukewarm water is hot and cold.

Warm water

Where Now?

This amazing trick shows that your sense of touch can be confused as easily as your sense of sight. Try this out with a friend.

Ask your friend to close her eyes and extend her bare right arm in front of her, palm up. Next, ask her to touch the back of her elbow with her left hand. Even with her eyes closed, she should have no trouble finding this spot. Now, tell your friend that you are going to touch her arm, starting at her wrist and gradually moving up towards the elbow crease. Ask her to tell you when she thinks you've reached the crease in her elbow.

Using just one finger, lightly trace overlapping circles that travel up your friend's arm. Move your finger a little more closely as you approach the crease in her elbow. She will probably tell you that you have reached the crease while your finger is still an inch or two away from it. When she does, ask her to open her eyes and see where your finger actually is. She will be amazed!

Ask your friend to try the trick on you afterwards. You'll probably be fooled too, even though you know what's going to happen! The phantom sensation that your friend is touching the crease on your arm is too real not to believe!

How the trick works
That phantom sensation is a result of "neural sensory overload"! This means the nerves in your arm that report to your brain have become overstimulated by the constant tiny circles that your friend is tracing on your arm. So they begin to tell your brain that you're being touched higher up on your arm than you actually are.

Cross Your Fingers

Here's a simple trick that is sure to amaze you and your friends.

Cross your fingers—your index finger and middle finger—just as if you were crossing them for luck, and close your eyes. Now, touch your crossed fingers to the tip of your nose. Doesn't it feel weird? Some people who do this trick report that their nose feels unusually lumpy and bumpy. Others say they have the illusion that they are touching two objects, not one. Try it!

How the trick works

When you cross your fingers, the parts of your fingertips that are usually on the outside are now on the inside. The part of your skin that is touching your nose is not used to this new arrangement, and it keeps signalling to the brain that something "on the other side" is being touched. Your brain interprets this information and decides that you must either be touching two different curved surfaces or one very bumpy one!

The Curious Coin Trick

A coin is round, isn't it? Well, this trick makes you think it's oval!

First find a coin one inch (2.5cm) or more in diameter. If you don't have a large enough coin, you could use a plastic disc, such as a poker chip. Grasp the coin between the thumb and index finger of your left hand and turn it with the thumb and index finger of your right hand.

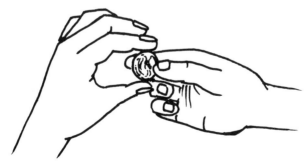

Turn the coin as quickly as you can. You'll get the strange impression that the coin is not circular, but is in fact an oval lying on its side. This illusion works best if you close your eyes.

How the trick works
It's all in the way you turn the coin. When you grasp the coin between the thumb and index finger of your right hand and rotate it, these two fingers are almost constantly in touch with the large, flat sides of the coin. This gives you a strong impression of the width of the coin.

By contrast, the height of the coin is not so clear, because the fingers of your right hand are only touching the thin edges of the coin.

Since, with your eyes closed you cannot see the coin to confirm that it's really circular, your brain accepts the idea that the large, flat sides of the coin are longer than the coin is high.

That Finger Weighs a Ton!

Stretch out all the fingers of one hand, except your middle finger, which you tuck up under your hand.

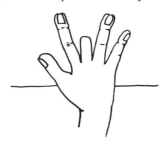

Then place your hand so that the rest of your fingertips are touching the tabletop. Now try wiggling your outstretched fingers. You'll find that you can move your thumb, your index finger and your little

76

finger easily, but when it comes to your ring finger, it's a different matter. For some reason, you'll find it very difficult—if not impossible—to lift it. You may experience the illusion that it is just extremely heavy, when it really weighs no more than your index finger.

How the trick works

Your middle finger and your ring finger share the same tendon, so it's very easy to bend them both at the same time. But lifting your outstretched ring finger while your middle finger is bent puts a strain on the tendon that they share.

Doing the Twist

This stunt should prove that even though you've lived with your fingers all your life, you still don't know everything about them.

How to do the trick

Hold your arms in front of you with your elbows bent and your upper arms vertical, as if you were holding a heavy bar level with your forehead. Then bring your right arm over so that your right elbow is sitting in the crook of your left elbow. Now bring your right wrist behind your left arm and clasp all your fingers together. Ask a friend to point to one of your fingers. Try to move that finger. You probably won't be able to move it the first time that you do this trick. You may think that you're moving the correct finger, but actually find that you're moving a finger on the other hand. If your friend touches the correct finger, it may help your poor, confused brain identify which finger it is supposed to move.

How the trick works
The trick works by confusing your brain. Normally, your right hand is on the right side of your body and your left hand is on the left. But when you twist your arms and fingers the way you do in this trick, nothing is normal, and your brain becomes confused.

You can see for yourself that it is the unfamiliar position that is confusing your brain by practicing the trick for a while. The longer your practice, the easier it gets to identify which finger you need to move.

The Illusion of Weightlessness

If you've ever worked out in a gym, done a lot of heavy lifting, or held your arms up for a long time, you'll know what it's like to have arms that feel as heavy as lead. Well, here's a trick that will convince you that your arms are lighter than even a feather.

How to do this trick
Stand in an open doorway and press your arms against the sides. Count to 60 slowly as you do this. Make sure to press outward as hard as you can. When 60 seconds have passed, step out of the doorway and into a clear space that is free of obstacles. You'll find that your arms mysteriously rise up as though pulled by some unknown force.

How the trick works
After their mighty effort pressing against the sides of the door, your arm muscles have not yet had time to "switch off" and relax. So they continue to lift your arms outward and upward, after you have stepped clear of the doorway.

7. Everyday Illusions

The Onion-Carrot Trick

Your senses of sight and touch are not the only ones that can be fooled. You can fool your sense of taste and smell as well. For example, you can trick your friend into thinking that she's eating a piece of onion when she's really eating a piece of carrot.

How to do the trick
While your friend is in another room, cut a very thin sliver from a fresh carrot. Then cut a slice of onion.

Return to your friend and put a blindfold over her eyes. Then, hold the slice of onion underneath your friend's nose and place the piece of carrot between her lips. Ask her to eat the food that you have placed in her mouth, and to tell you what she thinks it is. She will probably reply that she thinks she's eating an onion. Then remove your friend's blindfold and show her that she has been eating a carrot all along. She will be amazed.

How the trick works
To understand how this trick works, you have to know how you taste and smell things.

When you taste something, tiny amounts of food that have been dissolved in saliva go into your taste buds—the little bumpy patches on your tongue. Inside the taste buds there are tiny little taste cells that have hairs in them. They send messages to your brain that identify what you're tasting.

When you smell something, molecules of that substance dissolve in the watery mucous at the top of the nose. The dissolved smell reaches your smell receptors, a patch of tissue full of nerve endings. They send messages to your brain that identify what you're smelling.

Your sense of smell is a lot stronger than your sense of taste. It is a vital part of enjoying the food that you eat. That's why, when you have a cold, you often find that your food loses its taste. When your friend eats the carrot thinking that it's an onion, it's because the weaker messages sent by your taste buds are masked by the more powerful messages that your smell receptors send to your brain.

Crazy Glass

Glass can bend light in some surprising ways. For instance, if you were to see a straight-haired friend standing behind a bevelled glass door, you might be fooled into believing that she had just gotten her hair permed. It will look crinkly through the bevelled glass because, as we saw earlier, light waves travel at different speeds through different substances and surfaces that are at different angles.

When the light waves enter or leave a substance that has a different density or thickness, they bend slightly (it's refraction again). When your friend's hair looks permed, it's because the light waves have been bent at slightly different angles by the different thicknesses of glass.

What Do You Really Look Like?

When you look at your face in the mirror, you see an image that looks like you—but you don't see what you really look like. To see the same view of yourself that other people see, you have to use not one mirror, but two. If you hold the first mirror in front of your face, and then hold the second mirror so that it reflects your image from the first mirror, then what you see in the second of the two mirrors is what you really look like.

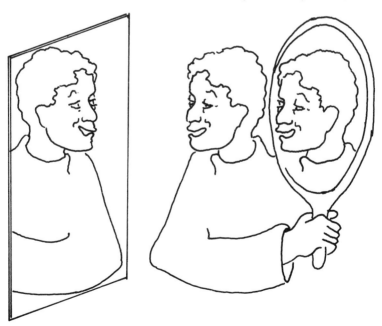

There are other images of yourself that are even less true to life than your mirror image. Hold up a shiny spoon and look into its hollow dish. Your reflection will look back at you—upside down. If you look at the other side of the spoon—the side that bulges out— you'll find that the reflection of your face also appears to bulge outward around the middle—and it's distorted in other ways, too.

Both of these images are illusions caused by the way that the light rays are bent when they strike the curved surfaces of the spoon.

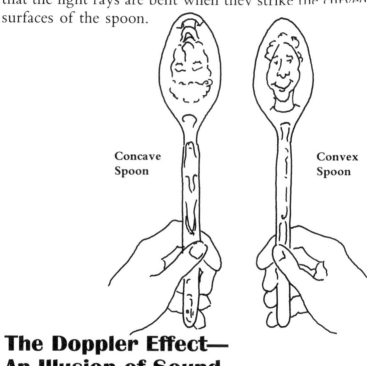

Concave
Spoon

Convex
Spoon

The Doppler Effect—
An Illusion of Sound

Have you ever stood on the street as an ambulance or a fire engine rushed past—siren blaring? If you have, you might also have noticed that the siren sounded different when it was coming towards you than it did after it passed and was speeding off into the distance. This is called the "Doppler effect."

Another example of this strange phenomenon is the way the sound of a car's engine seems to change when it approaches and then passes you at high speed. If you ever thought that the change in the car engine was due to something that the driver was doing, such as changing gears or putting his foot down hard on the gas pedal, you were wrong. The change in sound was actually a common audio illusion.

How it works

The reason why noisy things sound different when they approach than they do when they pass you has to do with the nature of sound.

Scientists describe sound as waves travelling through a substance such as air or water. There are three different factors that determine what a sound is like. These are its length, known as wavelength; how fast it's travelling, known as the speed of the wave; and how often the waves are produced, known as the frequency.

When waves are produced by an engine, they spread out and travel through the air in a circular pattern, rather like the way ripples spread out around a stone you throw into still water.

If you're standing next to a parked car that has its engine running, you can think of each sound wave as a pulse of energy that travels through the air until it reaches your ears and you are able to hear it. Each wave of sound that reaches you has the same wavelength. It has the same speed and follows the previous wave after the same time interval, so the frequency of the sound waves is the same. Therefore, you hear the sound the engine makes as a constant noise.

When a car is approaching you, however, it's a different matter. The frequency of the sound waves increases. This is because when the car is moving toward you, it is also moving towards the sound waves sent off by its engine.

Imagine, for example, that a car is speeding down an empty road, its engine sending off a sound wave. By the time the engine sends off its next sound wave, the car is starting to catch up with the first sound wave. Then, by the time it sends off a third sound wave, the car is catching up with the second sound wave it produced.

As the car continues to travel towards you, this pattern continues, so that the sound waves that reach you are closer together: they arrive at a greater frequency.

When the car passes you and moves away into the distance, the opposite effect takes place. The sound waves you hear are those that spread out and travel away from the car in the opposite direction from the one the car is taking.

Imagine, now, that the car's engine sends off a sound wave that travels towards you as the car drives off into the distance. When the engine sends off the next sound wave, it will have farther to travel than the first sound wave in order to reach you. This pattern continues as the car races off into the distance. The individual sound waves that follow have farther and farther to go before they reach you, so you hear them less often. Their frequency decreases. It is this decreasing frequency of the sound waves that causes you to hear a change in the sound of the engine.

Wacky Wheels

Next time you see a cyclist pedalling by really fast, take a good look at the wheels on her bike. If you watch the spinning wheels carefully enough, you'll think they are spinning backwards! Then you will once again see them spinning forward in the direction that the bike is travelling.

How the illusion works
The reason that the bicycle wheels sometimes appear to be spinning backwards is really quite simple. It's because they're revolving so quickly that your visual system just can't keep track of what they're doing.

Your eyes and brain can only process a certain number of images each second. They can't really cope with any more information.

In the case of the spinning bicycle wheels, your brain stops trying to follow the forward motion of the spokes and starts following how many complete revolutions the wheels make instead.

When the spinning bicycle wheels don't appear to complete a full circle (a 360° revolution), your brain interprets any shortfall as backwards motion.

Which Way?

When you're travelling in a car at high speeds on a highway, you might come across this peculiar illusion.

If you sit in the backseat of the car and look out the side windows, you can experience the very strong feeling that the cars going in the opposite direction are whizzing past terrifically fast and the car that you're in isn't moving at all.

It's a lot like another famous illusion: sitting in a stopped train while watching a neighboring train start up—and being sure that your train is moving.

How the illusion works

The reason that you sometimes feel as if you're not moving—although you're travelling along at a high speed—has to do with the way your brain adapts to your environment.

You've probably noticed, for example, if you visit friends who live in a noisier neighborhood than yours, that while the traffic may sound very loud to you, your friends no longer notice it. They have lived with the noise long enough to have become accustomed to it. Their brains "tune out" the noise.

A similar thing happens to sailors after they've been at sea for a while. They automatically adjust their stride to compensate for the swaying of their ship. When they first disembark, they may walk with a strange rocking motion for a while until they adjust to the fact that the land doesn't sway from side to side the way their ship does.

After you've travelled in a car for a while, your body and brain adjust to the motion of the car and tune it out, so you feel as if you're not moving. And since you feel as if you're not moving when in fact you're going

60 miles (96km) per hour, the cars going in the other direction seem to whiz by twice as fast. This is because the combined speed of both cars moving away from the point where they passed each other is 120 miles (192km) per hour.

Ping-Pong Blank Out

For an extremely interesting way to experience how your brain "tunes out" constant stimuli, try the following experiment.

Take a Ping-Pong ball and cut it in half with scissors, making the edges as smooth as possible. Then lie down in a quiet, dim place, and put one Ping-Pong ball over each eye. Simply gaze up into the dim whiteness of the hollow shell and let your thoughts drift.

At some point, while you're staring into the Ping-Pong balls, you will probably experience what is known as "blank out"—the experience of not seeing. Your sense of sight will seem to literally disappear. You won't even be able to tell whether your eyes are open or closed!

Scientists who have studied this phenomenon report that although the visual information from the inside of the Ping-Pong balls reaches your retina, it disappears in your brain! Because the visual information never changes, your brain just ignores it.

Some people have reported that in addition to not seeing, they also experience dream-like images.

After trying this experiment, you may find that you feel very relaxed. While you were in the "blank out" state, your brain waves changed from faster beta waves to slower, and to more powerful alpha waves, which are associated with relaxation and accelerated learning.

Down the Road

You may have experienced this optical illusion when you've travelled down a long, straight, flat road—or looked down a straight section of railway tracks. In both cases, even though you know that the edges of the road and the railway tracks are evenly spaced, they don't look as if they are. As you look farther off into the distance, the road or the tracks seem to get narrower and narrower. If you could see far enough, the two lines would seem to meet and the road would disappear.

How the illusion works

The reason that things in the distance seem to be smaller than things that are close to you has to do with the way that your eyes and brain calculate size.

In general, the size of the angle made between the edges of the thing that you're looking at and your eyes determines how big or small the object seems to be. The farther away the object, the smaller the angle. The closer the object, the bigger the angle.

You can test this out. Take a piece of paper and draw a horizontal line three inches (7.5cm) long at the top of the page, parallel to the top edge of the paper. Now find the center of this line and mark it with a tiny dot.

Measure two inches (5cm) down the paper from the center of the line and draw another, larger dot. This dot represents the front of your eyes.

Next, draw two lines from this dot to the ends of the horizontal line. You will have an upside-down triangle. The angle between the two slanting lines and the dot that stands for your eyes is called your "angle of vision."

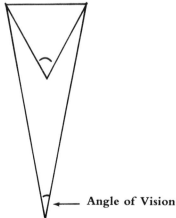

Now measure about six inches (15cm) from the horizontal line, and mark that point with another dot. This dot also represents the front of your eyes, but this time they are farther away from the horizontal line. Connect this new dot to the horizontal line to form another upside-down triangle.

You will see that the angle formed at the bottle of this triangle is much smaller than the first angle.

Now you can see for yourself that when you look at things that are close to you, you've got a larger angle of vision than you do with things that are farther away.

Next, imagine that the lines that form the sides of the triangle cross each other when they enter your eye, so that they form an X.

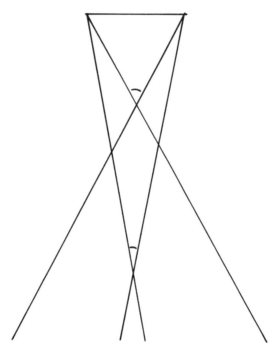

Look at the difference between the two X's. With the wide angle of vision, you get a wider space between the arms of the triangle than you do with the narrower angle.

These measurements correspond, in a simplified way, to the images formed on your retina—the screen at the back of your eye. The line that represents the closer object has a larger angle of vision—so it forms a larger image on your retina, and it looks larger to you.

Mirages

When crossing a burning hot desert, thirsty travellers often say that they can see a lake full of cool, shining water. But when they rush to the place where the lake appears to be, they find it isn't there at all. Their wonderful vision of refreshing water has been only a mirage—a natural optical illusion.

You don't have to live in the desert to see a mirage. Often on hot summer days in the city you can look down the street and see what looks like a pool of water shimmering in the middle of the road. If you take a closer look you find that the road is completely dry. The pool of water was only a mirage.

Mirages are caused by that process we talked about before called "refraction." Because light travels at different speeds through different temperatures, it actually bends from its straight line path and travels to your eye at a different angle.

When this happens, you are receiving a "false" message, and you can be fooled into thinking that the image is real.

Answers to Hidden Pictures

1. The showman's wife is actually the showman's dog. The dog's front legs form her legs, and the dog's fluffy tail forms her head.

2. The cat is hidden between the two left-hand branches of the tree.

3. The donkey is hidden between the two women.

4. The table is the cup. Its handle is formed by the back of the chair on the right-hand side.

5. The houses at the top of the picture are built on top of the giant's nose. The small forest to the right forms his eyebrows. The enclosure near the middle of the picture forms his ear, and the large patch of forest forms his beard.

6. Turn the book upside down and you will see the landlord's face in what has become the far left-hand side of the picture, between the ground and the branches of the tree.

7. The butler is hidden in the dog's coat. Turn the page upside down and you will see that the dog's left-hand shoulder is also the butler's chin. The butler's nose extends under the dog's left arm.

8. The doctor's face is hidden behind the cat's back.

9. One child's face is hidden in the top of the mother's hat. Another child's face is hidden in the shoe, just above the tray that the woman is carrying. (This face is upside down.) Another child's face is hidden below the shawl that the woman wears around her shoulders, and another bulges out of the back of her apron, just below the bow tied around her waist. The face of the last child is hidden in the hem at the bottom of her apron.

10. The rats' faces are hidden in the cat's ears.

11. The dog's master is hidden in the dog's face. Turn this picture upside down and you will see that the part of the dog's ear hanging down past the far side of the dog's face forms the man's hat. The man's bearded face and hair are hidden on the lower part of the dog's face, between his nose and eye.

12. The patient is standing behind the nurse, wearing a shirt with spots on it. The patient's head is directly behind that of the nurse.

13. Captain Webb's face is hidden in the cliff at the left-hand side of the picture. The bottom of his nose is about an inch below the bottom of the two pine trees.

94

14. Turn the book so that the queen is lying on her front, and you will see the king's head in what is now the top right-hand corner of the picture. His arm stretches down towards the bottom of the picture, and his legs extend up to the queen's head.

15. The tree behind the goat forms the milkmaid's hair. The goat's tail and back leg form the silhouette of her nose, mouth and chin.

16. The rabbit has hidden itself cleverly on top of the cook's head, in his hat, the last place that he would think to look for it.

17. The bird is hidden in the top left-hand portion of the picture. The bird's beak and breast are defined by the outer curves of the two baskets in the left-hand side of the drawing. The bird's eye is the little bump on the side of the stick in the top left of the drawing.

Index

Alpha waves, 88
Angle of vision, 88–90
Artificial pupil, 9, 13
Baseball mitt, 48–49
Beta waves, 89
Bicycle wheels, 85
Blank out, 87–88
Blind spot, 50
Bridge, rebuilding the, 50–51
Coin trick, 43–45, 75–76
Cole, Edward William, 28
Cole's Funny Picture Book, 28
Color Viewing Box, 58–60
Doppler effect, 82–84
Escher, Maurits, 26
Eye movements theory, 71
Finger lift, 76–77
Good continuation, 14, 15, 17
Gregory, Richard, 71
Hidden pictures, 28–37
Impossible figure, 25, 26, 27
Lens; convex, 62; in eye, 5
Light: and dark, 15, 16; colored, 56–57; waves, 57, 80–81
Magic tricks, 63–69
Magnifying glass, 61–62
Mirages, 91
Mirrors, 82–83
Moire effect, 24
Muller-Lyer illusion, 69–71
Neural sensory overload, 74

Optical distortion, 9, 11, 12, 13, 20, 22, 27
Optic nerve, 6, 50
Pencil tricks, 46, 64–65
Penrose and Penrose, 26
Ping-Pong ball, 83–84
Prisms, 53–54
Pulsating designs, 9
Rainbows, creating, 51–54
Refraction, 44, 54, 62, 91
Retina, 6, 50, 65, 90
Reversing figure, 22
Scarf trick, 63–64
Shadow illusions, 36–42
Smell, sense of, 79–80
Sound, illusion of, 82–84
Sense of, Stereokinetic effect, 21
Sunlight, 54
Tactile illusions, 69–78
Taste and smell illusions, 79–91
3-D Viewer, 60–61
Transparency, 24
Tricks, optical illusion, 44–63
Water: hot and cold illusion; trick, 66–67
Wave, alpha, 88; beta, 88; length, 83–84; light, 57, 80–81
Weaknesses in visual system, 5, 8
Weightlessness, 78
Zollner effect, 18, 19